LORE *of the* GREAT TURTLE

INDIAN LEGENDS OF MACKINAC RETOLD

written and illustrated by
DIRK GRINGHUIS

MACKINAC STATE HISTORIC PARKS

i

Printed by Harlo Press, Detroit, Michigan
1st Edition: 10,000 copies
2nd Printing 1973: 10,000 copies
3rd Printing 1978: 10,000 copies
4th Printing 1984: 10,000 copies
5th Printing 1992: 7,500 copies

LORE *of the* GREAT TURTLE

CONTENTS

Dedicated to my Indian and non-Indian Friends

at

Holy Childhood of Jesus School

Harbor Springs, Michigan

ALGONQUIN INDIAN SUPERNATURAL BEINGS

in order of importance

Git-chi Man-i-tou: The Great Spirit, maker of all things.

Mit-chi Man-i-tou: Spirit of evil.

Ka-be-yun: Ruler of the West wind.

Ka-be-bon-ni-ca: The North wind.

Wa-bun: The East wind.

Man-a-boz-ho: Son of the *Ka-be-yun* and a mortal. *Man-i-tou*, trickster, sometimes a fool. A favorite subject for lodge stories.

I-a-goo: Teller of tall tales.

We-eng: The bringer of sleep.

Pau-guk: The spirit of death with a skeleton body and burning coals for eyes.

Kwa-sind: The strong man who helped clear the streams and the land.

Puk-wudj-in-i-nees: Little people or fairies of the land.

Wen-di-goes: Cannibal giants.

Red Gee-bis: Cannibals also, Sorcerers, magicians, necromancers.

v

BIRTH OF THE ISLAND

1

For countless years Mackinac* Island, Michigan was viewed with awe by the Chippewa, Huron, and Ottawa as well as by their enemies the Iroquois to the east, the Sioux to the west. Approaching the island in their canoes they were filled with superstitious wonder at the tall rocks each bearing a spirit of a mighty *Man-i-tou*. And it was here that the Great Spirit, *Git-chi Man-i-tou*, who had formed the island, dwelt alone except for the giants in the rocks. Here he accepted the sacrifices and offerings. Here also were buried the dead chiefs and their families that they might be forever under his protection.

Most believed the island was created for this very purpose. Long ago the Chippewa tell of fishing in these very waters before there was such an island. And then, they said, there came a great fog which shrouded the Straits of Mackinac for three suns. When it rose there lay the island with all of its trees and blooming flowers. It was at that time that *Git-chi Man-i-tou* came to stay.

For many moons no one dared venture near. But finally they came to timidly offer gifts of wampum and other treasures to do him honor. In return he filled their canoes with fish and their lands with game. It was he who gave their chiefs the gift of speech, the warriors strong arms, the arrow makers skill in working the flint.

* pronounced Mack-inaw

But one day the white man came. Then, seeing the harm wrought upon his people, *Git-chi Man-i-tou* fled in anger and sorrow to the frozen north as the caribou had done before him, to live forever in the flickering flames of the Northern Lights.

This is only one legend collected by the famous Henry Rowe Schoolcraft who in 1820 served as superintendent of an expedition for discovering the sources of the Mississippi River. Geologist, author, explorer, he gained an international reputation for his collection of legends of the American Indian, a collection that served as the base for the epic poem, "Hiawatha" by Henry Wadsworth Longfellow.

In 1820, Schoolcraft was appointed Indian Agent with headquarters at Sault Ste. Marie. Later he moved to Mackinac Island where he lived for eight years collecting further Indian material as well as helping to build an Indian Dormitory providing food and shelter for Indians who came on government business.

Today the Indian Dormitory has been restored. Schoolcraft's office, the kitchen and other features of the building are viewed by thousands of summer visitors yearly. The building also houses a fine Indian museum with artifacts, murals, and dioramas depicting this colorful era in the history of the Island.

Schoolcraft's success as a biographer of the Indian was due not only to his careful attention to detail but to his deep sympathy for these first Americans whose ancient culture and rituals were being slowly destroyed by encroaching settlers and traders. He speaks of their beliefs as to the origin of the earth, the Great Spirit, and the creation of man and the animals with understanding and admiration.

Many of the following collection of legends are retold from his works.

MICH-I-BOU AND THE FIRST MAN

2

Long, long ago, the Great Hare called *Mich-i-bou*, sat with all his creatures on the surface of the water. In appearance he was unlike anything seen by man. He had four legs, two of which were used as arms. So, it was said, he had four legs and two arms but there were only four in all.

Each of the others were different in form. Some had only one leg, others ten or even twenty. Others had no legs only arms, some had none at all. The number of eyes and noses also varied. But strangest of all was the Great Hare, father of all creatures on the waters.

The wife of *Mich-i-bou* was as strange looking as he and bore him many children. One day as she was about to deliver his thousandth child, she had a dream that the unborn child demanded a solid place on which to stand. When she told her husband he was puzzled. But at last decided he would create such a place and diving beneath the water brought up a grain of sand from the bottom. Holding it in his hand he blew upon it until it grew into an island. He set it afloat and here the first man was born. He was given the name of *A-to-a-can* meaning, "Great Father", and he was a giant who towered above the tallest trees.

Soon *A-to-a-can* grew lonely. The flowers springing up, the trees laden with fruit, the bushes heavy with ripe berries failed to please him. At last he put clay upon his head and called out to his father, the Great Hare.

"I am lonely, *Os-se-maw*, Father," he cried. "Give me someone to share this place."

Mich-i-bou who had now gone up into the sky to watch, heard him. Looking about among the people of the air he saw a lovely maiden who name was *A-ta-hen-sic*. She was bright as the sun, beautiful as the moon, and playful as the whirling stars.

When the Great Hare asked if she would like to make a journey to earth, she, as all women who are offered a journey to a new place, was happy to try this new life with the handsome young giant below. And so, *Mich-i-bou* using the sinews and tendons of land animals, made a long rope on which he lowered her to the lodge of his son.

Now *A-to-a-can* was happy. He could now leave to hunt the deer knowing his wife would be waiting for his return.

In time a boy and girl were born. When they grew up they married and built a new lodge away from their parents. Others were born and grew tall.

One day, *Mich-i-bou* himself descended to earth to see how the population of the world was growing. Seeing only a few people, he instructed his son and grandson in another method. Upon the death of any animal they must skin the animal and burn the skin. Next they must take a drop of their own blood and place it upon the carcass which then must be covered with forest leaves. On the fourth day when the leaves were removed they would find an infant who would cry out in delight at having become a human. Having told them thus, *Mich-i-bou* went once more up into the sky never to return.

A-to-a-can and his sons did as they were told and soon there were many new people on earth each made from a four-footed animal.

And thus it is that people even today, bear the marks of their animal being. Some are swift and crafty, they are of the red fox. Those with red skins like the moose are brave. Others with white skin are cowardly, their ancestor

6

is the rabbit. Some are great leapers, they came from the mountain lion. Others, clumsy and slow, came from the muskox, while bloodthirsty warriors are descended from the wolf. This explains the ways of men; brave, cowardly, fierce, timid, all inherited from the animals that gave them human life.

SUGAR LOAF ROCK

3

Man-a-boz-ho was, to the Indian, a person of miraculous birth who served as a messenger of the Great Spirit. He was believed capable of superhuman feats, yet at the same time was a man with man's weaknesses and foolishness which brought him much closer to the Indians themselves. There are many legends of his battles with monsters, he is swallowed by a great sturgeon and escapes, his magic canoe carries him anyplace he wills. In addition he can speak to all the birds and animals and receives their council. He destroys fearsome serpents or evil giants and is talked about in every lodge during the long winters. And, this prophet and trickster is said to have spent his early life among the people.

First, he is brought up as a child and learns man's customs. He takes a wife, builds a lodge, hunts and fishes, sings his war songs and medicine songs, goes to war. He suffers defeat and victory. Sometimes he wanders half starving. Because he lives the lives of the people, his magic powers are never beyond the belief of the people themselves.

In the following tale we learn of his old age on Mackinac Island. And while some say that Sugar Loaf Rock was the wigwam of *Git-chi Man-i-tou* himself, this legend gives another version.

Man-a-boz-ho was old. Now was the time to sit before

9

a warm fire and relive the adventures of his youth untroubled by the strife of his people. Here on this island where the first humans were born, *Man-a-boz-ho* sat before his lodge, pipe in hand. Beyond the flicker of his fire lay the broad waters of Lake Huron empty except for the moon path that silvered its waves.

But many moons to the south there were those who wished that he had stayed among them. Ten of these were young men who, as children, had listened to the story tellers weaving their magic with tales of the brave and foolish deeds of the mighty *Man-a-boz-ho*. Now as young men, the ten wished to find this great magician so that he might grant each the special wish they held deep in their hearts. Finally they banded together, determined to seek him out.

For five moons they travelled over places where other moccasins had not trod, places haunted only by spirits. They fought the churning waters of mighty rivers in their birch canoes and scaled great rocks at the carrying places. At last they came to the broad water where far on the horizon lay an island shaped like a sleeping turtle.

Wearily they started out in their long canoes to what they hoped would be the end of their search. Four times they started and four times they were turned back by the water spirits who sent huge waves across their bows. Then on the fifth day after scattering tobacco on the face of the water, they found the Straits of Mackinac calm, the sky a friendly blue.

Eagerly they dipped their paddles until they drew close to the great rocks of the Island. Only then did they pause, for this was a sacred place. Summoning up their courage they at last drove their canoes onto the beach and started in single file toward the rocks and forest above them.

It was there they found him. An old man whose long hair bore the mark of winter snow, seated in front of his lodge.

One who served as leader, moved forward and placed his gifts of tobacco and wampum on the deer hide upon which the old *Man-i-tou* rested.

10

"We have come, *O-me-shaw-me-see-maw*, grandfather, to ask a final boon that we may be men among men. Will you grant our wishes."

Man-a-boz-ho bent his head, nodding, so that his eagle plumes tossed in the lake breeze.

"*Ne-ga-wob*, I shall see," he answered and his voice was like *Ke-nu* the Thunderbird at a great distance.

The first youth then asked that he be turned into a great war chief that he might drive the enemies to the east and west from the lands of his people.

"Your wish is granted," said *Man-a-boz-ho*. "Return to your village where one day soon your very name shall bring weakness into the bellies of your enemies. Your war club shall strike like lightning, your arrows sting like *Au-mons* the hornet. One day your belt will be heavy with trophies and your eagle feathers countless. Men shall sing your name across the land."

The second wished to be a great hunter. Again *Man-a-boz-ho* granted the wish, saying:

"You may return to your village. There, soon, there will be none to surpass your skill at tracking whether it be across bare rock or rolling seas. Your bow shall be like the mighty oak, your arrows straight, your eyes like those of *Pen-ay-see*, the hawk. Go, my son, and may you never know hunger."

The third asked to be a powerful shaman or medicine man. Again the old man agreed.

"You will read the dreams of your people and cure their wounds. You will cast spells or remove those placed by evil magicians. Your medicine bundle shall be filled with magic."

The fourth asked to be a strong dancer, imitating the eagle, *Wing-ge-zee*, or *Me-shay-wog* the elk. The fifth asked to be an orator speaking wise words for all to listen; the sixth a teller of legends; the seventh a maker of swift canoes; the eighth the handsomest of braves; the ninth the fastest runner and the strongest in games. And *Man-a-boz-ho* granted them all their wishes.

Now when it came time for the tenth to ask his secret

11

wish, all grew silent, wondering.

The tenth youth stepped forward and placed his gifts. Then he spoke.

"I wish, oh mighty *Man-i-tou*, that I may never die but that I shall live for all time."

Across the wrinkled face of *Man-a-boz-ho* passed a cloud like that cast when a flock of *Awn-day-gog*, crows, flies low over the earth. Raising his hand that held the pipe he pointed the stem straight at the tenth youth.

"Now, I am angered," he said, and the nine braves trembled. "You have asked the one gift no mortal can have. But, because I have given my word that all gifts be granted eternal life is yours."

While the others watched they saw their friend grow, twist, change shape, until he became a tall rock.

There he stands today, unmoving, in sun, snow and storm, viewing the lake with eyes that cannot see. He that had been given eternal life was without life forever.

ARCH
ROCK
4

T his strange rock formation was looked upon with awe
by the Indian as the bridge over which departed souls
could find their last resting place in the Island caves. As to
its creation, there are many legends. This one tells of a
mortal woman and her love for a sky spirit.

Along the beaches on the shores of Lake Huron dwelt
a band of Chippewa (Ojibway). Their lodges, round topped
and fashioned of saplings and elm bark, lay peacefully beneath the forest boughs.

In the finest lodge with its door blanket of moose hide
dwelt the chief of the band and his beautiful daughter called
She-who-walks-like-the-mist. When she carried water from
the lake in her clay vessel or worked the bright designs of
dyed moose hair and porcupine quills into soft moccasins,
the young braves watched with admiring eyes. But Mist
Woman paid little heed. Her work days were long without
a mother to help. But she never complained and her father
was proud. Some day, he knew, she would marry a fine
brave from another clan and bear him many sons.

At first when the young men began coming to their
lodge bringing gifts, Mist Woman smiled and offered them
wild rice that she had gathered in her canoe.

Then one day all was changed. Suddenly the young men
found her sitting with downcast eyes instead of welcoming

smiles. As her father saw her drawing more and more apart, paddling in her canoe alone at night, he became angry.

"Why, *Ne-daw-niss*, my daughter, do you who once smiled on the strong young men who brought you gifts, now treat them with a cold heart. Are you under an evil spell."

Mist Woman only shook her head.

"A daughter cannot always dwell in the house of her father. You must choose a husband soon or you will become old and wrinkled like *Mez-he-say* the turkey."

Still his daughter was silent.

In anger the father rose and picked up a heavy stick from the ground. "I have never beaten you, daughter. But I shall unless you tell me why you refuse my wishes."

Slowly the girl lifted her head. She saw anger in her father's eyes. At last she spoke.

"It is true my father that I am under a spell, but not the spell placed by a sorcerer."

"What then." asked her father fiercely.

"Let me speak that you may know my heart. Often when I go to gather the wild rice it is late and often the star path of the dead is in the sky when I return. Two moons ago as I paddled to the eastern shore of our village a handsome brave appeared to me. His clothing was of the whitest deerskin covered with designs my fingers have never made and my eyes have never seen. But even more wonderful was his robe of shining light. I tried to paddle quickly homeward as a daughter should, but my hands were helpless and my canoe drifted. It was then that he spoke to me. 'Oh lovely one,' he said. 'Long have I watched you in the village wishing that you might be mine for all time. In my home high above you I am the son of a chief, Evening Star, and am therefore a Sky Person. And so I felt I dare not speak to you of my love. Then, as I watched the young men coming to your lodge bearing gifts, my heart felt heavy and I became as one without hope. It was then that my father came to my couch of bird feathers and I told him of your beauty. He understood and gave me leave to descend to earth that I might ask you to join me in my sky home.' ''

"And what did you answer, my daughter."

"I said that I would marry no one but him," Mist Woman answered.

"*Kau-win!* No! It is forbidden. You shall marry no one at all!"

Seizing her by the arms, he shoved her roughly out of the lodge toward the lake shore. He placed her in the bow of his war canoe and with mighty strokes drove the craft straight to the Island of the Turtle Spirits. There, he drew out a long cord made of deer sinew and throwing the noose about Mist Woman, dragged her toward the great rock which towered above the beach. There he tied her hand and foot. "Now," said he, "you shall not see your lover again. Here shall you lie until you decide to be a faithful daughter once more." And off he strode.

Mist Woman made no answer nor did she cry out when the sun grew hot or the rain beat upon her helpless body. Only her tears flowed down upon the rock, speaking of her longing.

Little by little the tears began to melt the stone until at last an arch appeared beneath her and she was left on a high bridge. That night through the arch appeared the rays of the evening star and down these rays strode her star brave.

Gathering her into his arms he carried her up the star rays into the land of the Sky People.

The tears that could not melt a father's heavy heart melted the stone on Mackinac Island.

THE
DEVIL'S
KITCHEN

5

It was the time of the Traveling Moon and the people gathered up their goods that they might move to the mainland for winter hunting. While the men readied the long canoes, the women made their way to the beach carrying sleeping skins and clay pots and food for the journey. At last even the sacred bundles had been removed from the island camp. By afternoon a long line of birch canoes headed south toward the mainland.

Near the Cave of the *Red Gee-bis* who were *Wen-di-goes* or cannibal giants, a girl watched the departing canoes. The man beside her, was old and blind. It was he, the old one, that the tribe had deserted. His granddaughter, young and beautiful, had stayed behind to care for him.

"My child," said her grandfather. "You should have gone with our people for it is there that your young man *Kee-we-naw* will seek you."

"He will find me, grandfather, though I were hidden in the deepest cave."

The old man shook his head sadly. Well he knew the dangers that surrounded them. Now blind and helpless, he could only hope that *Git-chi Man-i-tou* would protect them.

"Do not despair," said his granddaughter who was named Willow Wand. "I have placed a white deerskin with vermillion markings high on the cliff. The fishermen will see it and come to our rescue."

The old one said nothing. Enemies might see it too. Him they would kill but he did not fear death although *Pau-guk* the death spirit was said to have eyes like flaming coals. It was for his granddaughter that he worried lest she serve out her years as a slave.

Sensing his thoughts, the girl took him by the hand and led him to a high ledge fronting a cave. Here she made him sit that they might await the canoes of the fishermen. Then gathering up their few sleeping skins and pots of clay and birchbark baskets, she set about making camp being careful to stay out of sight of the caves called the Devil's Kitchen where the *Red Gee-bis* dwelt. True, there was great danger at night if they were seen by these torturers and eaters of human flesh. Still, enemy warriors were unlikely to come to this spot for they too feared the red devils.

At last the cave was ready and as Willow Wand sat about the evening meal of a small handful of corn, she saw a movement far back in the cave. Seizing a blazing stick from the fire, she stood with hard-beating heart as a huge black shape moved toward her. It was *Mag-wah* the she-bear. Slowly the girl backed out onto the ledge.

"What is it, child?" asked the grandfather.

"Yaw! It is *Mag-wah!* If I am quick perhaps I can kill her with your bows and arrows."

The old one raised his sightless eyes. "Let us all live in peace. Let her sleep in her lodge that we may sleep in ours."

Almost as if she understood, the she-bear turned on her flat paws and disappeared back into the cave.

Together the girl and her grandfather lay down to sleep after eating their scanty meal. The girl in the cave dreamed of her beloved. The old man stayed on the ledge, wakeful. At last he sat up and fumbled in his tobacco pouch for his *ki-nick-i-nick* or tobacco. A few crumbs remained and these he carefully tamped into the stone bowl of his pipe. Lighting it from the fading fire, he next laid out his medicine bundle and carefully unwrapped it. Food was running low, he could tell from the lightness of the food bag that Willow Wand had eaten but little. And water was scarce. To go to the lake after water now would be sure to invite the terrors of the Red Giants.

Slowly the sun sank and the coolness told the old one of the coming of night. With it, he knew, would come the cries of the tortured ones waiting to be roasted above the cooking fires in the caves below. The old man did not fear death, he had lived too long among wild beasts and painted warriors, but now with his blindness he feared that he could not warn his granddaughter of danger. Reaching out he touched each item of his medicine bag, praying for strength.

A whimpering came suddenly from inside the cave. The grandfather listened. It came again. *"Au-pet-chi-ne-guskaw-nawgwe . . .* I am very thirsty."

It was Willow Wand pleading for water in her sleep. As he listened, helpless, he thought back to his daughter, mother of Willow Wand, who at her deathbed had whispered this secret to him. The girl had inherited a magic gift from her father, a gift which if used rightly would give her the powers of a medicine woman. She would then gain fame as a healer and prophet, for unknowingly she had the power to bring springs of pure water from the earth in any quantity she desired. But, her mother had said, she could not be told of this power until she had undergone the seven days of fasting to become a woman. Only then could she be told.

Now, the old man wondered, if perhaps this might not be the time, for was she not without water and food?

From the caves below came the cries and moans of the tortured captives and the smell of roasting flesh. Even through his blind eyes, the grandfather thought he could see the red flames.

At last the singing of birds told him of dawn. The caves were silent but still the old one refused sleep.

For seven days and nights it was thus, the grandfather sleepless, guarding the cave entrance, the girl crying out for water in her sleep.

21

On the seventh night her cries grew louder. Painfully the old one made his way into the cave. As he did so, Willow Wand opened her eyes. Leaping to her feet she struck the rock with her hand and cried, "Water!"

Instantly, a tiny stream burst from the rocks. Willow Wand gave a glad cry and together they drank from the fresh clear stream.

Now, over a few kernels of corn, her fast broken, Willow Wand listened to the story of her gift. How it should be used for good and never in jest.

At last the old one's voice trailed off and he nodded in sleep. At the same time the girl thought she heard a voice saying, "*Yaw!*, there is danger!"

Gently she covered her grandfather with a robe that he might sleep. Then she knelt near the cliff's edge to watch.

From the Cave of the *Red Gee-bis* she saw the red glare of cooking fires followed by the terrible shrieks of the captives. Now, wakened by the sounds, *Mag-wah* the she-bear came out from her cave to stand close to the girl. Willow Wand felt no fear at the touch of the bear. Surely this is no regular bear thought she, but one bewitched by an evil magician into the bear shape.

Then across the round topped islands a storm arose tossing black clouds across the sky. Birds of evil shape sailed overhead and all living things on the Island fled for shelter. *Yen-add-i-see* the crazy gambler must be playing for high stakes, thought Willow Wand. For the winds were now fighting each other in this wild game and the score was being kept by the long lightning strokes.

Even louder than the wind rose the screams of the victims below. And then to Willow Wand's horror, she saw the figure of a young man being dragged, bound, into the evil cave. It was *Kee-we-naw*, her beloved.

Her cry of terror awakened her grandfather. As he sat upright, ready to defend his granddaughter he felt a cold muzzle at his ear.

"Fear not, Father," said the she-bear. "I am the spirit of thy daughter. Watch and fear not for my daughter, Willow Wand is now a woman with full powers."

It was then that the chief of the *Red Gee-bis* looked up and saw Willow Wand kneeling on the ledge. He held up his hand to stop the ceremonies for he recognized her as the holder of the wand of power and this he desired. As he did so, the girl saw *Kee-we-naw* edging back toward the cave entrance. In order to distract the *Gee-bis*, Willow Wand now rose to her feet and sent out peal after peal of mocking laughter toward the hideous red devils below.

It was then that *Mag-wah*, her bear-mother, turned and disappeared into the darkness knowing that all would be well.

Now the Devil chief began disguising himself that he might capture Willow Wand. In the next instant he appeared suddenly upon the ledge in the guise of an enemy warrior. In threatening tones he demanded the hand of Willow Wand. But she, piercing his disguise, laughed at him and ordered him gone.

In fury he leaped to the cliffs above intending to drop down and carry off the girl. But as he sprang, she struck the wall a mighty blow sending out such a gush of water that it flung the devil straight to the bottom of the Demon's Hole and quenched the fires of the *Gee-bis*. While the *O-kies* and the devils were trying in vain to rekindle their cooking fires, Willow Wand sent a rainbow mist to serve as a bridge and the next moment *Kee-we-naw* was at her side. Quickly she cut his bonds then handed him a tobacco pipe filled, that he and her grandfather might smoke together. For now it was dawn and time for her to complete her task. All that day she worked. Escaping demons who were drowned in the lake, the fires were put out forever and by nightfall the cave of horrors was empty.

At dusk she returned to her grandfather and to *Kee-we-naw*. It was then he told her of his search. How he had found their tribe to the south and how they had directed him back to the Island. It was there that he had seen the vermillion painted deerskin. But as he had started toward the beach a pair of beautifully decorated moccasins had floated by. Taking them from the water he had placed them on his feet and was instantly transported to the Devil's Cave.

The following spring, when the people returned, they found Willow Wand and her husband and Grandfather living comfortably in the cave. All winter they had been warmed by the firewood left by the *Red Gee-bis*.

Thus ended the terrors of the terrible *Wen-di-goes* and their abode where once they roasted and ate men, the Devil's Kitchen.

DEVIL'S LAKE

6

Near the shores of Mackinac Island, near the cave of the *Red Gee-bis*, there was once a bottomless lake. Here dwelt an evil *Man-i-tou*. It is said that the cold clear water that still drips from down the rocks once served the *Gee-bis* for their stews and although the water still drips, the lake itself is dry.

Long ago when the lake was full, the people feared going near because of the evil *Man-i-tou* living deep in the swirling waters. It was he who could sing sweet songs to lure unsuspecting children to his abode from which they never returned.

One day, Little Rail, whose name comes from the marsh bird, took a young bride from across the blue water. During the summer it was his wife's delight when not attending to the needs of her husband, to roam the Island. Unaware of the evil present at Devil's Lake, she approached it one warm evening that she might bathe in its cool waters. Above her the sweet boughs of cedar bid her welcome and the moss at the lake's edge was soft against her bare feet. Putting aside her robe of feathers, made for her by her mother, the young woman stepped into the pool. A strong swimmer, she launched herself into the deep part of the lake.

Instantly the sun seemed to hide behind the ragged clouds that quickly appeared and the small creatures scurried for shelter.

Fearing what seemed to be a coming storm, she climbed back upon the bank and hurriedly donned her feathered robe. But before she could gain the safety of the trees a bright flash of light revealed a terrible figure coming out of the lake while the once quiet waters lashed in torment.

In terror she tried to run but, to her horror, found that she could not move nor speak.

Now, moaning and shrieking, the evil *Man-i-tou* came toward her. Taller than any man he seemed to be made up of many beasts. From his head rose the palm-shaped antlers of the moose while his body was that of the wolverine and his feet those of a bear. Only his hands were human and from him shone a strange bluish light that flashed as he moved.

Striding forward he reached out and tore the feathered robe from the helpless woman.

"*Aee!*" he shrieked, "I now have the magic robe that was to protect you. But my magic is stronger! From this moment you shall serve not your husband in his lodge but me in my bottomless home!"

At this moment, Little Rail, hearing the cries of the monster and fearing for his wife's safety, came racing toward the lake. Seeing his wife in the grasp of the evil *Man-i-tou*, he called out with all his might, "*Pa-kau*, stop!" and began raining blows with his warclub upon the giant. But his blows were in vain. At last he fell exhausted upon the rocks, crying out to his wife to free herself and run to the sacred land of the village where no devil dared set foot. But the poor woman could only answer with her eyes for she could not move.

Now the evil *Man-i-tou* waved the feather robe three times above his head thus making her his complete slave. Next he released her and ordered her to dance for him. Knowing it was against tribal law to dance except for special occasions and feasts, the woman, feeling a slight movement returning to her arms and legs, went through the motions of a dance thereby hoping to escape. Displeased at so poor a performance, the wicked one reached out to sieze her. In despair she began the Death Dance. It was then the *Man-i-tou* lifted her in his arms and turned toward the lake.

In dismay Little Rail watched helplessly, fearing *Pauguk*, the death spirit, and he pleaded that his wife be returned to him.

But the evil one merely laughed. "I shall take her to my lodge beneath the water," he boasted. "She may return to you only when the lake is dry." And he tossed the helpless woman into the black waters where she instantly sank. Then the terrible *Man-i-tou* began throwing boulders on top of her that she might not rise. For hours he threw stones and rocks then turning toward the grieving husband he hurled a final stone that struck him between the shoulders making him a hunchback.

Little Rail struggled up and in desperation began also to throw stones and even pebbles after the disappearing monster. For even an evil *Man-i-tou's* promise is good and he knew if the lake became filled with stones it would become dry and his beloved would return.

At dawn he returned alone to his village to tell the sad tale. And so it was that his people, as well as other tribes who approached the lake, cast a stone into the lake that she might be returned to him.

Today the lake is dry and it is said that the young couple are thereby reunited. But even today, Little Rail, keeps his hunchback shape, a broken-backed little duck.

SKULL
CAVE

7

The great chief, *Ke-nu*, the thunderbird, was troubled. Long ago he had been a maker of peace pipes, molding them between his fingers from the red clay. During that time there had been peace within the tribe. Now that he had become a chief for many years, there was endless bickering which grew louder and more tiresome each day. It was time to consult *Mich-i-bou* the Great Hare for the answer. After speaking with the prophets, after fasting, he was ready.

Telling no one, he went first to the Red Clay Hill. Here, as of old, he took a great mound of pipe clay and went toward the Place of Skulls. There, in this sacred place, far from human haunts, he knew that *Mich-i-bou* would be waiting. *Ke-nu* was sure of this for he had taken daily gifts to the place and the *Man-i-tou* would be surely pleased.

Ke-nu knew he must find the way of peace for his heart was heavy. He, the Thunderbird, had been a great warrior but he had not become so by fighting with mere women. And yet the sound of their wrangling had grown so loud that he now eagerly sought the quiet of Skull Cave even though it contained rows of skulls and skeletons of dead warriors. Even the spirits of air and of earth had lacked the power to frighten the women in silence. Only *Mich-i-bou* could help him by turning the soft clay into true peace pipes so that the smoker might once more know true brotherhood.

When he reached the cave, he knelt, bending over the place of the sacred Medicine Bundle. As he waited for the voice of *Mich-i-bou*, he traced designs in the sand of the pipe bowls which he would make if the Great Hare gave his permission.

Suddenly a skeleton rolled toward him from the cave basin. *Ke-nu* drew back, afraid. But the skeleton spoke, saying:

"Do not fear me. Under thy feet you will find soft copper. Out of it I shall make tubes a pipe's length and in their sides pierce a small hole for a peace note. You may then place therein a reed that it make a sweet sound. Then shall you cover them with clay and place them to dry. Next with thumb and forefinger fashion the pipe bowls you have drawn." And the clacking voice of the skull grew silent.

Eagerly *Ke-nu* set to work. As had been spoken he found the soft copper beneath his feet. This the skeleton fashioned into pipe length tubes and pierced them for the peace note. *Ke-nu* placed the reed, then covered them with clay and set them out to dry. As soon as they were ready the skeleton blew into the holes making each note one of sweetness and power, working each until each was as sweet as the first. Only then did *Ke-nu* turn the pipe bowls between thumb and forefinger and join them to the stems. Rising to his feet at last he bent and placed a pipe in the jaws of each of the skulls that they might have a trial smoke. In return for this courtesy, the skulls gave each pipe great drawing power which long afterward men tried to copy and failed.

Ke-nu gave the sacred pipes to his people. Again there was peace in the village for after drawing upon the pipes, the skeletons became living men and took wives from among the women who ceased their quarreling.

Thus the Cave of the Skulls became the Cave of the Peacemakers.

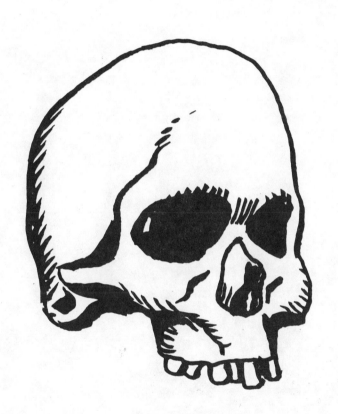

LOVER'S LEAP

8

High above the Island on a lonely rock sat *Lo-tah*, beautiful daughter of the Chippewa. Below her stretched the blue waters where dwelt *Maw-may* the sturgeon, *Au-saw-way* the perch, and *Au-de-kaw-meg* the whitefish. Here also dwelt the terrible underwater panther. But *Lo-tah* thought not of these things. Instead her dark eyes sought distant specks that would tell her of the return of *Ge-niw-e-gwon*, the young brave whom she loved and planned to marry. It was many moons ago that he had left to gain more eagle plumes by defeating the enemy to the east. Thus did he hope to prove his worth so that the father of *Lo-tah* might think him a mighty warrior, fit for a son-in-law. As she watched the empty sea, as she had done each day since he left, *Lo-tah* hummed a love song of her people:

> "A loon, I thought, was looming,
> A loon, I thought, was looming,
> Why! it is he, my lover,
> Why! it is he, my lover,
> His paddle in the waters gleaming.
> His paddle in the waters gleaming.

Suddenly something moved toward the horizon, small specks that turned into a flotilla of canoes. As they neared the beach, she heard the warriors' voices raised in song.

35

Leaping to her feet she began to run toward the returning canoes. Then she stopped, and a cold chill came upon her heart. For the song was the death song! In vain she searched for a glimpse of her beloved. It was then her spirit told her that *Ge-niw-e-gwon* had gone to the Spirit-Land of the West.

It was true. A feathered arrow of the terrible Iroquois had found its mark, and after he had been placed against a tree facing his enemies, he died. But his last words were for *Lo-tah*.

For seven sleeps, *Lo-tah* remained atop the great rock. And seven times her lover appeared to her as a beautiful bird. At last she knew the time had come to join her beloved. On the morning of the eighth day her father found her crumpled body at the base of the rock. *Lo-tah* had taken the trip of the souls to be joined forever with her love. Since that time, the rock has been known as Lover's Leap.

THE GIANT'S FINGERS

9

L ong, long ago at the beginning of Time, the Island of the Dancing Turtle Spirits was the home of a band of red-skinned giants. When the time came for them to leave the earth they became waiting spirits. Others were turned into wandering demons according to the will of *Git-chi Man-i-tou*, the Great Spirit. The waiting spirits became rocks or pinnacles or boulders. The demons appeared as men with heartless and cruel souls.

There was one giant who refused to become a rock or a man but instead tried to go down into the Under Land where dwelt some of the spirits of the dead. He chose a crack in the island for his descent, not knowing it had magic powers having been created by *Git-chi Man-i-tou* himself. This crack in the Island lay in a place of dark shadows and sad cries, a crack of sheer rock with no footholds where some had fallen on dark nights never to return.

Now, this foolish giant in trying to descend, found his fingers frozen to the mouth of the opening in punishment. There he was doomed to hang for all time, dangling over the terrible dark below.

Beneath the scaling limestone it is said that his hands may be seen today. Should anyone tread on these immense stone fingers, they are instantly smitten with misfortune. For while the giant is powerless to move, he still holds terrible powers which he does not hesitate to use.

Whence came the crack in the Island? It is said that it was created by *Git-chi Man-i-tou* before he fled to the Northern Lights. It was here that he stamped his foot creating the great crevasse (where the giant dwells) when the white man came to the Island. And it is said that on the day that the Great Spirit completes his spells, the crack will split and fall apart. Thus shall the island sink once more that the red-man may prevail.

THE
VOICE
OF
THE
GREAT
TURTLE

10

It was summer, and on Mackinac Island the people knew it was the time for the asking ceremony. Soon they would gather up their mats and their medicine bundles, their pots and sleeping skins, their bows and arrows and clubs for hunting and for war. Then they would load their long canoes for the trip to the hunting lands farther south. Now was the time to find out where the beaver and the deer would be found and where might lurk the enemy, waiting to fall upon them and carry off the young women of the tribe.

So it was that the men of the village took their stone axes and went into the woods. When they returned, they had five tall trees with the branches removed, one tree of each kind of wood to be found. These they lashed into a wigwam which pointed to the sky. Next moose hides were brought and stretched about the wigwam, covering all but a few feet at the bottom so that the tribe could watch the ceremony.

That night when the moon was full, the tribe gathered with their children and formed a great circle about the pointed lodge. Only then did the *sha-man* or medicine man appear. As he strode into the firelight, the people grew hushed for his magic was great, his prophesies true. Some of the smaller children hid their heads for he was terrible

43

to look upon. Crowning his long black hair (which was worn in the manner of the *sha-man* and not shaved to a scalplock) rose the feathers of the great blue heron, while the long beak stuck out in front. His face and body were painted, one side red, the other black, with white circles around his eyes. And through his nose was thrust a polished deer bone. In one hand he carried a snapping turtle rattle using the dried neck as a handle. In the other he held his drum. From his belt hung his medicine bag made of otter skin decorated with quills of the porcupine and dyed moose hair, and on his feet were moccasins also decorated. The *sha-man* stopped quickly and seated himself in full view of the people inside the wigwam. Suddenly the entire wigwam began to tremble and then shake violently until the pointed tip seemed almost to touch the ground. Then terrible voices came from somewhere both in and outside of the wigwam, the mewing of puppies, the cry of terrible birds, screams, roars, howls. Only then did the voice of the turtle speak high and faint. One by one the warriors moved forward with gifts of tobacco to ask the future. Each time the *sha-man's* spirit answered, sometimes flying to distant places to seek knowledge. At last it was over and the people returned to their sleeping skins.

This was the lodge-shaking ceremony of the old times, a ceremony witnessed by the white man after his coming, an unsolved mystery of the Indian.

THE SUMMER MAKER

11

Once on the shores of the Straits, lived a great hunter whose name was *O-jeeg* meaning Fisher. So strong were his powers that many thought him to be a *Man-i-tou*. He lived in a wild and lonely spot with his wife and a son of thirteen. Great were his hunting skills, and he almost never came back to the lodge without venison or some other game for his family. His son, watching, determined also to become a mighty hunter. Taking his bow and arrows he ranged far from the wigwam seeking small game. But at that time a deep snow lay over all the land and the air was bitter cold. Try as he might, the boy's half-frozen fingers could not draw the bow to its proper length nor could he hold the arrow against the string. Many moons he tried but at night he returned without game to huddle in his sleeping skins and weep.

One day as he made his sad way homeward without a single animal at his belt, he saw *Au-san-aw-go* the squirrel atop a pine stump. Fitting an arrow to his bow he moved stealthily forward. But as he raised the bow, the Squirrel began to speak.

"Do not shoot me, oh grandchild, that I may give you advice. Day after day I see you returning weeping from the terrible cold. If you will listen exactly to what I say, we shall both enjoy summer forever. Then you will be able to

47

find food for in this snow I am starving."

Eagerly the boy dried his tears and moved closer to the squirrel, his bow forgotten.

"When you reach your lodge," continued *Au-san-aw-go*, "weep louder than ever before. You must throw your bow and arrows away from you. If your mother asks why, say nothing but continue to weep. Should she offer you food, refuse it. When your father returns he too shall ask the cause of your grief. Only then may you answer, telling him that the snow is too deep and the winds too cold. You must then stop your crying and plead with him to melt the snow so that you may become a great hunter also."

The squirrel continued. "Your father will then say that what you ask is very difficult but that he will try by using all of his powers to grant your wish."

The boy agreed and hurried home. He did as he was told and everything happened as the squirrel had prophesied.

So it was that his father set about making a feast. A whole bear was roasted and to the feast he invited his friends Otter, Beaver, Lynx, Badger, and Wolverine. After the feast, all prepared for a long journey and after three days *O-jeeg* took farewell of his wife and son, knowing he would never see them again, and he departed.

For nineteen sleeps they travelled meeting with no misfortunes. On the twentieth day they reached the foot of a high mountain. Here they found tracks of some person who had killed an animal for there was blood on the snow. *O-jeeg* told the others to follow the tracks that they might find food and after a time they all sighted a lodge hidden at the mountain's foot. Now *O-jeeg*, the Fisher, (which is a small and quick animal) said they must be very serious and not laugh at anything they saw. They agreed and stepped close to the lodge. The door skin then lifted and revealed what looked to be a man yet his limbs and body were so distorted that it was impossible to tell who or what he was. His head was huge, his teeth and eyes very strange and he had no arms. They wondered to themselves how he killed his game. When he told them he was a powerful

Man-i-tou, all accepted his invitation to spend the night in his wigwam.

Once inside, the *Man-i-tou* boiled the meat in a strange hollow wooden vessel then took it out in some manner unknown to them. Next he portioned it out to the visitors but his movements were so strange and humerous that Otter, the jester, burst out laughing. With a terrible look the *Man-i-tou* leaped straight on top of Otter intending to smother him as this was his way of hunting. But Otter slipped free and fled with the curse of the *Man-i-tou*. The others remained the night and talked of many things. At last the Fisher told his son's wish. The *Man-i-tou* agreed that it might be done but that it would cost *O-jeeg's* life. Thinking of his son and wife, *O-jeeg* agreed. Whereupon the *Man-i-tou* told them what they must do and the road they must follow.

Next morning they set off, meeting Otter who was waiting cold and hungry. Fortunately Fisher had brought some cold venison and so they continued for twenty days until they reached an even higher mountain. This they climbed and by nightfall had reached the top. They paused then to rest and smoke. But before smoking they followed their usual ceremony of pointing to the heavens, the four winds, the earth and the zenith. Speaking in a loud voice all asked the Great Spirit that their mission be fulfilled.

Above them the sky seemed very close. After smoking all prepared themselves. *O-jeeg* told Otter that he would be the first to try. Otter agreed and gathering his muscles made a tremendous leap at the sky but fell back to earth. There, the snow being moist, he slid down to the foot of the mountain (a thing otters still like to do to this day.)

Next came the Beaver who failed, then Lynx and Badger. All fell senseless in the snow.

Now *O-jeeg* turned to the Wolverine. "It is up to you," he said. "Your ancestors have long been known for their strength and cunning. It is you who must make the try."

Wolverine agreed and gathering his strength, leaped straight at the sky. Back he fell only to try again and again.

Now *O-jeeg* could see that the sky was beginning to give way.

"Once more!" cried Fisher.

On this try Wolverine broke through and went in and Fisher followed.

They found themselves on a wide plain covered with all sorts of beautiful and sweet smelling flowers. The air was warm and the sun shone on sparkling lakes and running streams. Birds sang everywhere. In the center of the plain were long lodges. Upon entering one, Fisher and Wolverine found them empty except for *mo-cuks* or cages of different sizes. Each cage held a different type of bird. Thinking of what fine hunting they would give to his son, Fisher cut open the *mo-cuks* freeing the birds who instantly flew through the hole in the sky and disappeared. Now the grasses and trees started to sway as the warm air began flowing through the hole toward the earth.

Suddenly there were shouts as the sky dwellers saw their birds and warmth leaking out. But it was too late. Spring, part of summer, and autumn had all gone. But before summer could completely escape, the sky dwellers separated it with a blow so that only part of it got away. Even then the ends were so mangled that whenever constant summer lies on a land it is always sickly.

Now, Wolverine, fearing for his life, ran to the sky hole and disappeared but *O-jeeg* kept opening more cages for his son. Too late he saw his escape cut off. Changing himself into his animal body, he ran across the plains of heaven until he reached a tall tree which he climbed. The sky dwellers followed and shot at him with arrows. But his body was safe against them except for one tiny spot at the tip of his tail. In vain he pleaded for his life with those who bore family totems the same as his. At last an arrow found the fatal mark. Weak from loss of blood *O-jeeg* fell to the ground. Stretching out his limbs to the north, he spoke his last.

"I have been faithful to my son and I die in peace. For I know that I have brought good to my people. Hereafter you may see me as a sign in the sky reminding all that it was I who gave them eight to ten moons each year with no snow."

Then he died. But in the heavens may be seen his constellation, the Fisher, with an arrow sticking in his tail.

THE
SEASONS

12

L ong, long ago, at the time of the Turtle Spirits, *Man-a-boz-ho* and his brother, *Pee-pauk-a-wis*, decided to run a great race. From the first, as always in contests of strength, *Man-a-boz-ho* was first, easily outdistancing his brother. As he ran, the sun shone warm upon him, the leaves spoke to him from the tall trees while the rabbit, the beaver, the deer, the fox, and all of the birds greeted him with glad calls. "Here comes the mighty *Man-i-tou*, our friend, who brings us fine weather," they said.

All summer long he ran northward, and each day was warm with sun. But *Pee-pauk-a-wis*, angry at being outrun, doubled his efforts and began to catch up. Then he noticed that wherever his brother's moccasins touched, flowers sprang up and the land was at peace with the sky. It was then that he grew jealous and decided to punish the earth. So he scooped up water in his hand and flung it into the air calling upon the Northwind and the Eastwind to make bad weather. Then he told the Southwind to first blow a great dry heat across the land to wither the wild rice and the growing corn. Then the Eastwind would bring rains to flood the rivers. Next he caused the clouds to blot out the sun that *Man-a-boz-ho* might lose his way. But *Man-a-boz-ho* needed only to look back and smile, and the clouds disappeared. It was then, in anger, that *Pee-pauk-a-wis* called upon the Northwind to bring hail and sleet and snow.

It was now that *Man-a-boz-ho* reached the Great Lakes. Here he paused to rest after his long journey. And there *Pee-pauk-a-wis* dashed past him in the night followed by the wind's fury. Realizing he had been tricked, *Man-a-boz-ho* leaped to his feet and overtook his brother, for a few short days that have become known as Indian summer. But then, winter at last settled over the land. Thus it is that, when the weather changes quickly as it does in Michigan, the people say that *Man-a-boz-ho* and his brother, *Pee-pauk-a-wis*, are running their race.

THE
CORN
SPIRIT

13

It was Spring and the eldest son had come of age. It was now time for him to undergo the ceremony called *Ke-ig-u-ish-i-mow-in* or the time of fasting. Only thus could he find his guardian spirit to guide him through life.

A lodge was set up for him away from home where he would spend his seven days without food or water, waiting for his unearthly visitor. The boy entered alone and began his fast.

For the first few days he walked in the woods and near the cliffs, gathering ideas which might appear to him in his dreams to come. As he walked, he saw the plants and flowers growing without man's help and he wondered. Some were good for food, some for medicines, some were poisonous. If *Git-chi Man-i-tou* gives us all things, he thought, why must we depend upon game alone for food? For if the game is scarce we go into our sleeping robes with empty bellies. Resolved to think of this he returned to the lodge, faint from thirst and hunger, and lay down.

That evening he awoke to see a tall brave coming toward him from out of the sky. He was dressed in yellow and all shades of green. From his scalp lock rose great plumes also of yellow and green.

The stranger raised his hand. "I am called *Me-daw-min*," said he. "I have come in your fasting time with a message from the Great Spirit who makes all things on earth and in the sky. He has listened to your thoughts and knows that you wish to give a gift of food to your people that they may not go to their lodges hungry. Arise now and wrestle with me that your wish may be fulfilled.

The young man forgot his weakness. And as he felt the courage rising in his heart he rose, determined to wrestle this spirit and thus gain his ends.

Back and forth they wrestled, sinew against sinew, until at last the stranger drew away.

"It is enough," said he. "Your heart is strong and tomorrow I return for another test."

The next day at the same time and place the green and yellow clad stranger reappeared. This time the youth felt even weaker but rose once more and siezed the spirit around the waist attempting to bring him to the ground. But once again his heart was stronger than his body and again he stood panting while the stranger spoke:

"Tomorrow will be your last test. Be ready." So saying he again disappeared.

On the third day when the stranger appeared at the same place and same time, again the youth forced himself to rise, determined to vanquish his opponent or die. Across the forest floor they wrestled until at last the stranger drew apart. "You have won," he declared. "Now listen to me closely." Together they entered the lodge and the youth sank to his mat to rest while he listened.

"Tomorrow," said *Me-daw-min*, "is the last day of your fast. When your father brings you food in the morning, do not eat nor shall you tell him of our contest. For I shall reappear once more for the very last time to wrestle. If you win once more, you must then pull off my garments of yellow and green. Then you must throw me to the ground and clear a space of roots and weeds. There bury me in the soft earth. Then may you leave this place returning only to clear the ground of grass and weeds. If you do exactly as I have told you, your tribe will know your greatness through that which you shall teach them." Once more the spirit disappeared.

In the morning the youth's father appeared with food and water.

"Eat and drink, my son, for you are weak from fasting. It is not necessary that you give up your life, this is not required but only that you learn of your future and the future of our people."

"My father, I thank you," said the youth softly. "But I must wait until sundown to partake of food."

"Very well, my son," answered the father. "I shall await you at our lodge with food and drink." And he departed.

For the last time the sky spirit, *Me-daw-min*, reappeared. Now the youth felt superhuman strength flow through him as they wrestled across the clearing. Suddenly the spirit grew limp in the young man's grasp. Remembering all that had been told him, the youth stripped off the beautiful clothing then dropped the sky-spirit onto the ground. Next he cleared a path of earth and buried *Me-daw-min* there in the soft earth.

Carefully, thereafter, he tended the grave daily never speaking of the contest fought there. Finally at the close of summer the youth called his father after hunting and bade him follow. Together they went to the place where the fasting lodge had stood. In its place, in the center of the carefully weeded ground, rose a tall and graceful plant with silken hair, topped with nodding green plumes and bearing golden cluster.

"This is my friend, *Me-daw-min* the Corn Spirit. No longer need we sleep on empty bellies when game is scarce. For the plant here and others like it shall take care of us."

He then showed his father how to strip away the husks as he had stripped away the yellow and green garments. He then held the corn to the fire until it turned brown. Returning to the family lodge, they all partook of the new food and found it good and together they thanked the Great Spirit for the giving.

THE
TURTLE
SPIRITS

14

There once lived a chief in the north who had ten daugh-
ters, the most beautiful of whom was *O-we-nee*. One by
one all nine married except she, the youngest. Ignoring the
pleas of the young men and the wishes of her father she
went her own way until one day when she married a very
old man named *Os-seo*. Poor and scarcely able to walk, he
was met with loud jeers by the older sisters. But *O-we-nee*
only smiled. "Wait and see," was her answer.

Soon after this all were invited to attend a feast. As
they walked through the woods the sisters could not help
but pity *O-we-nee* who was as beautiful as her husband was
old and ugly. As they walked the old one kept his eyes on
the Evening Star and was heard to mutter: *"Sho wain ne
me shin nosa,"* meaning, "Pity me, oh Father."

"He is crazy," whispered the sister. "Already he sees
Pau-guk coming for him."

Suddenly they came to a hollow log pointing toward the
path. *Os-seo*, who was of the turtle clan, let out a strange
yell and dashed into the log. When he came out the other
end he was young and handsome. Like a young antlered
buck, he sprang to the head of the party to lead them. In
amazement the people looked at him and then at poor *O-we-
nee*. For she had changed into an old woman, bent nearly
double, and walking with a stick. Quickly *Os-seo* returned

to his wife, calling her sweet names and holding out his hand to help her as she had helped him during his enchantment.

Soon they reached the lodge where the feast was to take place. Here the host made a long speech telling them that the feast was in honor of the Evening Star, then the food was passed out according to age and character. All were happy except *Os-seo* who continued to gaze at the heavens. Suddenly from the sky came a voice that grew louder until all could hear.

"My son, I have seen your sorrows and I pity you." said the voice. "Now I come to call you from this land of blood and weeping. The earth is sorrowful. Giants and sorcerers roam the land bringing evil to the hunter and into the lodges of his family. But the spell you were under is now broken. Come up into the skies, ascend that you may share the feast I have prepared among the stars and bring with you those you love. The food before you now is enchanted and blessed. Fear not to eat it. This food shall give you immortality and the eating bowls will no longer be of wood and clay. They shall become of wampum. They shall shine like the fire and glow like vermillion. Your women shall no longer be doomed to labor but shall put on the beauty of the stars and become shining birds of the air clothed in bright feathers. They shall dance and not work, sing and not weep."

The voice paused, then continued. "My beams shine on your lodge with the power to change it into a cloud of many colors. Come, *Os-seo*, my son. Look steadfastly at my beams for my power is now at its height. Doubt not nor delay for this is the voice of the Evening Star."

Os-seo understood each word that was spoken but the others thought of them as distant music and the singing of birds. Suddenly the lodge began to tremble and rise into the air. Too late to run away, the people could only watch as it rode above the tops of the tallest trees. In amazement they saw their dishes change into glowing shells while the lodge poles shone like silver and the bark covering gleamed like the wings of insects. In the next instant brothers, sisters, parents and friends were transformed into birds of various plumage. Some were jays, some partridge some passenger pigeons. Others were song birds singing sweet songs.

Only *O-we-nee* kept her human shape, bent and old. Once more *Os-seo* cast his eyes pleadingly toward the sky and gave out his strange cry. Almost at once his wife's beauty and youth returned. Her garments were as shimmering water and her stick became a feathered wand.

Again the lodge shook for now they were passing through high flying clouds. Soon they found themselves in the lodge of Evening Star, father of *Os-seo*.

"My son," said the old man, "Hand me that *mo-cuk* or cage of birds which you brought, beside the door. I will then tell you all that has happened."

Os-seo did as he was told and he and his wife seated themselves in the lodge.

"Pity was shown you," said Evening Star, "because of your wife's sisters who showed contempt for you and laughed at her ill fortune in marrying you. You had been under the spell of the spirit who lives in the next lodge, that small star you see to the right. He has always been envious of our family because of our greater power and the fact that I am the Woman's Star and in charge of the female world. This wicked spirit in trying to destroy your relatives, instead turned both you and your wife into old and nearly helpless beings. You must be careful not to let the light of his beams fall upon you for they are his bow and arrows and his weapons of enchantment."

Os-seo and his wife lived happily in the star lodge and soon his wife presented him with a son who grew tall and straight, the image of his father. The boy soon learned many things and because he heard that hunting was a favorite pastime in the world below, begged for his own bow and arrows.

Os-seo made them for his son and then opened the cage of birds which he had brought that his son might have practice at shooting. One day the boy who had been aiming and releasing the swift arrows, brought down one of these birds. As he picked it up, he was amazed to see it turn into a beautiful young woman with an arrow in her breast. It was one of his young aunts. But the moment her blood spilled upon the star surface, the charm that held the youth was dissolved. He felt himself sinking, held up by invisible wings. Slowly he drifted downward until at last he landed upon a large, tree-covered island set in a blue sea. Looking up he saw his uncles and aunts following in the forms of birds while behind them came his father's lodge. Gently it landed atop the island and there they all took up their abode. Now, all returned to human shape but not human size. Instead they became *Puk-wudj-in-i-nees*, little people or fairies. And each evening they would dance across the rocks in honor of the Evening Star.

Thus it was that the people who dwelt below, saw that during the summer months, the rocks were covered with the dancing fairies and called them *Mish-in-e-mok-in-ok-ong*, or dancing turtle spirits.

Here the Island got its name, and when the white men came they called it in their tongue, *Mich-il-i-mack-in-aw*.

THE
ROBIN

15

An old man had a son of whom he was very proud. When the time of fasting came that his son might become a man, the father was determined in this pride, that his son should receive a more powerful guardian spirit than any in the tribe. He therefore bade the boy to prepare most carefully in the sweating lodge and that he bathe several times. He then told the boy he must fast, not for seven days as was the custom, but for twelve!

Not wishing to disobey his father and thereby bring sorrow into the lodge, the young man agreed. When the time came that his fasting lodge was built, he lay down upon his mat, covered his face and began his vigil.

Each morning his father came to him and urged him to continue fasting that he might bring honor to his tribe as a warrior, prophet, or hunter. After speaking at length he would go away. The son listened and spoke not a word Thus it continued for nine days.

On the tenth morning when the father appeared, the son spoke for the first time since the fasting.

"My father," he said, "my dreams tell of evil to come. May I break fast now and at some future time make a new fast?"

"Oh, my son," answered the father, "you know not what you ask. If you cease now all your glory will disappear. Wait but two days longer and I shall bring you food and drink that you may be a man!"

Silently the boy drew the covering over his face and the old man withdrew.

The next day the son again asked that he might break the fast until another time. Again the father spoke to him of the glory to come and went away. So it continued until the morning of the twelfth day. Elated that the end had come, the father prepared food and hurried to the lodge. At the door, he stopped for he heard his son speaking.

Kneeling, the father peered through the door and was astonished at what he saw. His son had painted his entire chest vermillion and was reaching as far as he could to paint his shoulders as well, and he was speaking, thus:

"My father has destroyed in his pride, my future as a man and has not listened to my pleas. He therefore shall be the loser for I shall take up a new state and be happy. I have not disobeyed my father but did as I was told. Now my guardian spirit has given me a new shape and a new life. Now I must go."

At this moment the father cried out, "Do not leave me, my son!"

But the young man flew quickly to the top of the lodge where he rested, turned into a beautiful robin redbreast.

Looking down at his father he spoke:

"Now I am called *Au-pet-chi*, the Robin. Regret not the change you see for I shall be happier than any man. I shall, however, always be his friend, staying close to his lodge not as a warrior but as a bringer of sweet sounds and peace. I am now free of the cares of human life. My food is close at hand in the fields and above the rocks. Farewell."

Then, delighted with his new wings, Robin stretched himself and flew into a distant grove.

THE RACCOON AND THE CRAWFISH

16

A-*se-bou* the raccoon was hungry. For days he had lurked near an island pool hoping for a tasty meal from *As-shog-aish-i*, the crawfish. But the crawfish knew he was waiting and would not go near the shore. Finally in desperation, the raccoon thought of a plan. Knowing that the crawfish loved to feed on worms he procured some wormy wood. With it he filled his mouth and his ears and spread some on his back. Then he lay down on the bank to wait.

After a time, an old crawfish approached the bank warily. As the raccoon did not move, he crawled ashore closer and closer, and then climbed over his ancient enemy. Thinking him dead, he called out: "Come, my brothers and sisters. The raccoon our enemy is dead. Come now that we may eat him!"

Hearing his cry, a great multitude of crawfish came climbing up the bank to nip with their sharp claws on their ancient enemy who appeared dead. Suddenly A-*se-bou* leaped to his feet and began killing and devouring until not a crawfish was left.

While he was still eating, a female crawfish with her little sister on her back approached the bank looking for her relatives. When she saw them all dead and dying, she resolved too that she must die. Marching straight up to the raccoon she said: "Here am I with my sister. We are now

71

alone in the world. You have eaten our parents and our relatives and our friends. Now you must eat us too." And she began to sing her death chant.

The raccoon felt shamed by this brave act. "No," he said. "I have eaten of the largest and the fattest. I will not dishonor myself with such little prey."

At this very moment, *Man-a-boz-ho* happened to be passing. Seeing what had taken place he cried to the raccoon, *"Tyau!* Thou art a thief and a merciless dog. Get thee up into the trees lest I change you into one of these worm fish. For remember you once had a shell and it was I who pulled three from the mud onto dry land. The *Man-i-tou* then took the poor little crawfish and her sister and cast them far out into the stream.

"There may you dwell," he said. "Hide there among the stones and hereafter you may be playthings for children."

THE WHITEFISH

17

In the ancient times there lived a famous hunter who had a beautiful wife and two handsome sons. Each day he went out to hunt, that his family might have meat, as well as hides for their clothing. The boys were left alone and amused themselves near the lodge playing games and practicing with their bows and blunt arrows that they too one day might be hunters like their father.

One day as they returned from a nearby woods, they saw a handsome stranger entering the lodge of their mother. They hid in the tall grass and before long the stranger reappeared only to dissappear into the forest. The next day he returned and the next, staying only a little while then leaving before their father returned.

On the fourth day they resolved to ask their mother who the stranger might be.

"Is it your father who asks" she said. "If he wishes I shall have the stranger return this evening. You are bad boys spying on me. It is not manly to lurk at home. Go into the forests with your bows and arrows that one day you may become men."

The boys were shamed and went their way saying nothing to their father.

Many moons passed and each day the stranger appeared. Again they resolved to ask their mother.

"Who is this man that walks not the forest trail and who carries no food or message."

Now their mother grew angry. "You will never be warriors thinking these lies." she said. "If you tell your father I shall be forced to kill you both."

Again the sons went into the forest but this time they went seeking their father. Late that day they found him next to a buck he had killed.

"Oh our father," they said. "We have waited too long in our uncertainty. Now we must tell you of the man who comes to our mother's lodge while you are hunting. Each day he arrives silently, carrying neither food nor message nor does he walk the trail."

Their father's anger was like the terrible *Wen-di-go* that fells trees with a single breath. Picking up his war club, stained red with the blood of the deer, he strode homeward toward his lodge.

The boys waited a reasonable time then followed. When they arrived at their home they found the lodge torn down, and their mother buried beneath the ashes of the campfire. Gathering up their belongings they moved to another place.

When the young men grew to manhood the sons were haunted by the spirit of their dead mother who appeared to them at night. Their dreams were terrible and they could not find sleep. Finally they and their father decided they must move to a far place and escape her evil spirit. And so they travelled to a place along Lake Superior where they built their lodge.

But the next morning as they approached the beach they saw a skull rolling along the sand. In great fear they dodged this way and that trying to escape. At that moment they saw a giant crane wading in the water.

"See, grandfather," they called out, "we are pursued by an evil spirit. Take us across the water to that humpbacked island that we might escape."

Hearing himself spoken to, the bird, who was of great size and age, stretched out his neck, bent his wings and landed beside them.

"I shall help you," he said. "But as you ride on my back be careful that you do not touch the spot on the back of my head. It is very sore and if you touch it I shall be forced to drop you into the water."

The father and his sons agreed, and all rode safely to the west shore of the island where they were put down.

The crane then flew back to his place along the shore. Now the skull cried out, "Oh, grandfather, carry me over that I may be with my children for I am sad."

The great bird flew to her aid, again saying that she must not touch the back of his head for the wound had not healed and was very sore. She promised, but as they flew she grew curious how such an ancient bird could have received such a wound and still live. As they were almost to the island she touched the spot. Instantly she was tossed onto the rocks below.

As the skull drifted in the eddies against the rocks, the brains scattered out into the sea.

From high above the crane spoke. "There you must remain," he said to the woman skull. "You have been no use during your life, perhaps now you may at last be helpful to your people."

As he spoke the brains began to form into fish roe or eggs and soon there was a new fish in the water of great whiteness and of a delicious flavor. Ever after it helped to feed the Indians of the lakes.

As for the hunter and his sons, they took the crane as their totem and their descendants use the mark for their clan even today.

THE MOOSE AND THE WOODPECKER

18

M*an-a-boz-ho*, master of the animals had killed the Prince of Serpents and now he was in great want. Gone were his magic powers, it was winter, and he had nothing to eat.

He said to his wife at last, "I think I will go walking and perhaps I will find some lodge with food to share." Some time later he came upon a lodge and the children playing ran inside to tell their parents that *Man-a-boz-ho* was coming for a visit.

This was the home of the red-headed Woodpecker. Upon hearing this, Woodpecker (who was a magician) went to the door of the lodge and invited *Man-a-boz-ho* in. After they had talked, Woodpecker said to his wife, "Have we nothing to eat? *Man-a-boz-ho* is hungry."

"No." answered his wife.

Whereupon Woodpecker rose to his feet then flew up onto a tamarack tree that grew in the center of the lodge. Then he commenced going up and down turning his head and driving his bill into the trunk. At last he drew out a fat raccoon and dropped it onto the floor. He then drew out seven more. These he dropped also then descended and said: "*Man-a-boz-ho*, this is all we have to eat. What else can we give you?"

"These will be good," *Man-a-boz-ho* answered and Woodpecker's wife skinned and roasted the raccoons. After they had eaten and smoked their pipes, *Man-a-boz-ho* rose to go.

Woodpecker said to his eldest child: "Give the rest of the meat to him that he may take it to his children."

As he was going out of the door, *Man-a-boz-ho* intentionally dropped one of his mittens. Before he was a long way off Woodpecker found it and directed his eldest son to hurry after the old man. "But do not hand the mitten to him," he instructed. "He is behaving strangely. Best to toss it to him."

The son did as he was told and *Man-a-boz-ho* said to him, "Is raccoon all that you have to eat?"

"No." answered the boy.

"Then tell your father to come to me with a sack," *Man-a-boz-ho* boasted, "and I will give him something to go with it."

When the boy returned with the invitation, Woodpecker turned up his nose. "What does that old one think he has?"

The next day, Woodpecker went to pay a visit to the old *Man-i-tou*. He was received with ceremony and then, *Man-a-boz-ho*, who had often boasted in the old days that he could do anything in the world that any animal or person could do, began to play the mimic, imitating Woodpecker's voice and manner. "Now," he said, "you shall eat what we shall eat." And thrusting a bone into his nose to imitate a beak he started to climb a tamarack tree that he had instructed his wife to set up in the lodge.

Man-a-boz-ho turned his head one way and another but each time he tried to climb, he would slip down. Finally he struck the tree so hard with the bone that he drove it up into his nose. Blood began to flow and he fell senseless to the bottom of the tree. Woodpecker ran out of the lodge and returned with his drum and rattle to cure him. As *Man-a-boz-ho* came to his senses he began to place the blame for his failure on his wife.

"She is worthless," he moaned. "Before I married her I could find raccoon anytime I pleased!"

Whereupon Woodpecker flew onto the tree and pulled

out five fat animals. "This is the way we do," he said, and left in contempt.

The snow continued and soon *Man-a-boz-ho* and his wife were again out of food. This time when he went walking he arrived at the lodge of Moose. Again the children playing outside saw him and hurried to tell their father.

Moose (who was a magician also) greeted him at the door and after they had talked he said, "Wife, what have we to eat. *Man-a-boz-ho* is hungry."

"Nothing," said the woman, who was decorating a moccasin with porcupine quills.

Whereupon Moose arose, undid the sleeve of his wife's dress and taking his knife, cut out a large portion of meat from her shoulder. He then applied medicine and that wound disappeared without a mark. The woman seemed not to notice anything at all and began to roast the meat over the fire.

After they had finished eating, *Man-a-boz-ho* dropped his mitten as before and left. Moose's eldest was told to return the mitten and to toss it in the air which he did.

"Wait," said *Man-a-boz-ho*. "Is that the only kind of meat you eat?"

"No," answered the boy.

"Tell your father to visit me and I will give him something special also."

"Ha!" answered Moose when his son returned with the invitation. "What does that old boaster think he has?"

But in a few days he took a cedar sack and went to visit *Man-a-boz-ho*. Upon entering the lodge, Moose saw that the *Man-i-tou* was imitating everything he had done even to his phrases and tone of voice. Finally *Man-a-boz-ho* undid his wife's sleeve and taking out his knife cut off a large piece of flesh never minding his wife's cries of pain until she fell to the floor from loss of blood.

"You are killing your wife, *Man-a-boz-ho*," said Moose and ran to his lodge for his rattle and drum. Soon he had restored her life and healed her wound. Now *Man-a-boz-ho* began to berate her saying she was worthless and before he had married her he had always gotten food in that manner.

Whereupon Moose took his own knife and cut a large portion of meat from his own thighs without pain or even a mark.

"This is how we do it!" he said in contempt and left the lodge.

Now *Man-a-boz-ho* was depressed. He sat silently with his head down. Several days he sat this way until he heard, like the sound of a wind, a voice which said, "Great *Man-i-tou* why are you sad? Do you not know that I am your guardian and that I will still help you?"

At once, *Man-a-boz-ho* took up his rattle and began a chant. After chanting for a long time he determined to fast. Blackening his face with charcoal he retired to a nearby cave telling his wife and children not to come near him. At the end of seven days he returned pale and thin. His wife then brought him food which he ate, made from roots which she had dug. When he had eaten he took his great bow, strung it and placing an arrow on the string sent the arrow straight through the bark lodge with the strength of a giant. "Now," he said to his wife. "Go outside where you will find a great bear shot through the heart."

She did as she was told and began skinning the bear that they might feast.

Next *Man-a-boz-ho* told his children to gather some red willow twigs which he cut into equal lengths. A red stick was then sent to each of his friends including Woodpecker and Moose inviting them to the banquet.

When they arrived all were surprised to see so much meat. As they ate, *Man-a-boz-ho* proud of his feast said, "*Aiee*. It is so cold and the snow is so deep that one can hunt nothing but squirrels. And this is what I have asked you to help me eat."

Woodpecker was the first to taste the bear's meat which looked so good. But before he could swallow, it had turned to bitter ashes in his mouth causing him to cough. Moose also fell to coughing from the mouthful he took and so did

82

the others. But each had too much respect for the host to complain, and so they kept eating and coughing until the lodge was in an uproar.

It was then that *Man-a-boz-ho* using his former power, as master of animals changed each into an *Ad-ji-da-mo* or squirrel. To this day these animals cough whenever anyone approaches their nests.

THE GOLDEN EAGLE

19

All of the birds of the Island gathered one summer's day to hold a contest. Each would attempt to fly to the sky world and the one that flew highest would win the prize. The first to try was the whitewinged gull. But while his wings were wide and strong he was used to soaring and so tired and came down. The next was the robin. Up into the air he went almost to the clouds, but he was too small and back he came. After him came the wide-winged heron, the small sparrow, the swift flying hawk and the noisy jay. At last only the eagle *Wing-ge-zee* was left. On soaring wings he circled higher and higher until he was almost out of sight. Satisfied that he had won he started down only to feel something spring from his back. It was a small gray linnet who had hidden there. Fresh and untired it soared completely to the edge of the sky world and returned.

Now a council was called as to who had won the prize. The linnet had flown the highest but he had not started from the earth as the others.

And so it was decided that the eagle had been the winner. Not only had he flown the highest of all of the larger birds, but he had been forced to carry the linnet on his back.

Ever after the feathers of the golden eagle have been the most honorable marks for a brave to wear.

ABOUT THE AUTHOR-ARTIST

DIRK GRINGHUIS was born in Grand Rapids, Michigan. His first drawing (at the age of three) was of an Indian canoe. Since then Michigan's early history, its pioneers, Indians, and soldiers have been a favorite subject for both his brush and typewriter. Since 1947 he has written 19 books for young people, ten on Michigan. Among them are *The Big Dig*, the story of archaeological research at Fort Michilimackinac, *Big Mac*, on the Mackinac Bridge, *Saddle the Storm*, adventure on Beaver Island, *The Young Voyageur*, Fort Michilimackinac and the massacre of 1763, and others. He is author-illustrator also of *In Grey-White and Blue, French Troops at Fort Michilimackinac 1715-1760* published by the Mackinac Island State Park Commission in their Mackinac History Series.

In addition to his books, Gringhuis is also Producer-Host for a weekly series of Educational Television shows on Michigan history for most of Michigan's elementary schools.

As an historical muralist he has painted over 15 murals for Forts Mackinac and Michilimackinac as well as drawings for the Indian Dormitory on Mackinac Island and for the Trader's House at Michilimackinac.

He holds special awards for his work on Michigan including the Governor's Award, and the Michigan Minuteman Award. He is listed in Who's Who in the Midwest.

Mr. Gringhius lives with his wife in East Lansing, Michigan, and is Curator of Exhibits for the Museum, Michigan State University.

SOURCES
for
LORE OF THE GREAT TURTLE

Blackbird, Andrew J., *History of the Ottawa and Chippewa Indians of Michigan* (1887).
Indian vocabulary

Kane, Grace F., *Myths and Legends of the Mackinaws* (1897).
Arch Rock, Skull Cave, Devil's Kitchen, Sugar Loaf, Devil's Lake, The Giant's Fingers

Williams, Mentor L., *Schoolcraft's Indian Legends* (1956).
The Summer Maker, Birth of the Island, The Corn Spirit, The Robin, The Raccoon and the Crawfish, The Whitefish, The Golden Eagle, The Moose and the Woodpecker

Wood, Edwin O., *Historic Mackinac* (1918).
Michibou and the First Man, Lover's Leap, The Voice of the Great Turtle, The Turtle Spirits.

Wright, John C., *Stories of the Crooked Tree* (1915).
The Seasons

INDEX

89